A First Book of
HAYDN

FOR THE BEGINNING PIANIST with DOWNLOADABLE MP3s

David Dutkanicz

Dover Publications, Inc.
Mineola, New York

All music available as downloadable MP3s!

Go to www.doverpublications.com/0486833259
to access these files.

Bibliographical Note

A First Book of Haydn: For the Beginning Pianist with Downloadable MP3s
is a new work, first published by Dover Publications, Inc., in 2019.

International Standard Book Number

ISBN-13: 978-0-486-83325-5
ISBN-10: 0-486-83325-9

Manufactured in the United States by LSC Communications
83325901   2019
www.doverpublications.com

Contents

Introduction

A First Book of Haydn continues the tradition of making musical masterpieces accessible for all levels. A wide variety of Franz Joseph Haydn's (1732–1809) compositions are presented here, many for the first time in simplified arrangements. Each selection has been specially prepared to introduce the beginner to this influential composer, aiming to develop technique as well as musicality from an early stage. Fingerings have been suggested, but should not be considered an absolute—each performer should feel free to customize to their needs. Phrasings and other markings have been kept to a minimum. These can be added as progress is made. Works are arranged in approximate order of difficulty, and are excellent resources for lessons, sight-reading, and personal enjoyment.

Air

This lovely melody is based on an old French *saison* ("seasonal" song) which Haydn was rather fond of. He adapted it for a number of works, most notably the Andante in A Major and the second movement of Symphony no. 53 ("L'Imperiale"). Play with a light character and even meter.

Moderato

Trio

from Divertimento for Viola D'amore, Violin, and Bass

Haydn wrote a number of works for a unique trio: viola d'amore, violin, and bass. The viola d'amore is a larger version of a violin with more strings and a deeper resonance. It was used primarily as a solo instrument in the generation preceding Haydn's Classical era: the Baroque.

Andante

Allegro
from 12 Little Pieces, no. 8

In addition to being a prolific composer, Haydn was also a famous teacher of both piano and composition. His most famous pupil was Ludwig van Beethoven. This is one of many exercises he wrote to practice both technique and musicality. The focus is on the third and fifth fingers of the right hand to play the melody smoothly and evenly.

Allegro

Fantasia

from String Quartet no. 65

This Fantasia has a tempo marking of "slowly and freely," which should not be interpreted as uneven and haphazard. Once the piece is at a solid tempo, add expressive nuances to the tempo. Note the triplet in the right hand of measure seven: evenly divide the notes into three equal parts between the first and second beats.

Slowly and freely

Benedictus

from Mass in Time of War

The original title of this work is *Missa in tempore belli*; ("Mass in Time of War"); however, it is also frequently referred to as the *Paukenmesse* (due to the prominent use of the timpani, or *pauken*, in German). In measure 17, bring out the melody in the left hand while keeping time with the repeated notes in the right, imitating a timpani.

Andante

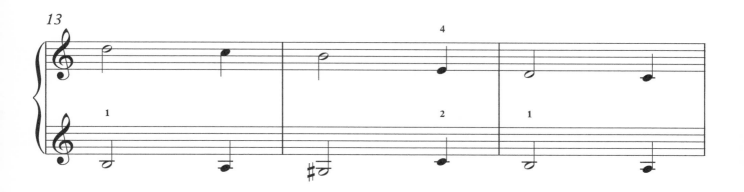

Allegro
from Cello Concerto no. 2

This moving melody opens Haydn's second concerto for cello and orchestra. It was dedicated to Antonin Kraft, the preeminent cellist of his day. Play at a tempo that propels the melody forward, with an even tempo throughout.

Allegro

Romance

from Symphony no. 85 "La Reine"

The fourth of the "Paris" Symphonies, this elegant theme is from a group of six symphonies commissioned by a French orchestra. *La Reine* is French for "the Queen," and that name was bestowed upon this work because it was one of Queen Marie Antoinette's favorites. Play gently and nobly.

Andante con moto

Kyrie

from Mass in Time of War

Haydn paints a musical picture of war in this movement. The peaceful first ten measures are contrasted by a sense of impending doom beginning at measure eleven. Note the use of Gb in measures twelve and fourteen versus the use of F# in measure 16; they are both the same pitch and key on the piano, but are spelled differently depending on their harmonic role.

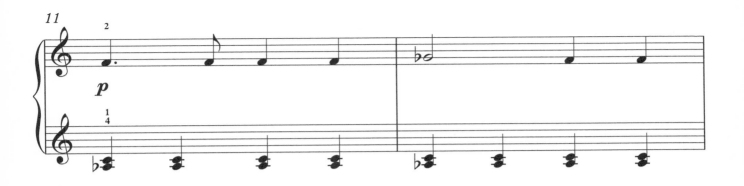

Hymn

This original melody was dedicated to Francis II, Emperor of the Holy Roman Empire at the time. After residing in London, Haydn wanted to compose something on par with *God Save the King*. It has since been adopted by Germany as its national anthem, and has been used in numerous hymns and at many official events.

Poco adagio

Symphony no. 94 "Surprise" (Opening)

Many of Haydn's symphonies are referenced by their nicknames. This symphony acquired its moniker by the jolting moments at the end of measures eight and sixteen. The composer wanted to shock his audience awake with unexpected accents, intentionally sedating his audience with a lullaby in the preceding measures.

Roxelane

A popular melody, Haydn adapted it a number of times: it was used as stage music, as a basis for piano variations, and as a theme for a symphony. When playing, keep the folk origins of the melody in mind and add extra accents on the first beat of each measure.

Allegretto
from String Quartet no. 74

This excerpt comes from one of Haydn's celebrated collections for string quartet. Pay attention to the thirds in the opening, playing them as one voice even as they are exchanged between hands.

Moderato

The Master and the Scholar
(Il maestro e lo scolare)

This charming work was composed as a theme and variations to be played by a student and teacher on one piano, four hands. The maestro ("master") plays a short phrase, echoed by the scolare ("scholar") an octave above. Try to imitate the musical material as closely as possible between the two voices.

Andante

Trumpet Concerto (Opening)

The Concerto for Trumpet is one of the most celebrated works for the instrument, and a cornerstone of the repertoire. It was written for a newly developed trumpet with an expanded range and new chromatic possibilities. Play with a shining tone and brass-like precision.

Allegro moderato

Seven Last Words Mvt. II

Haydn was a devout man, and found religious expression in his compositions. The title refers to the last words spoken by Jesus on Good Friday, and was originally written for orchestra (with a string quartet arrangement and choral version created later). The tempo marking implies a solemn tone, with an emphasis on the right hand to soar above.

Grave e cantabile

Aria

from Creation

Originally entitled *Die Schöpfung* in German, this oratorio depicts the creation of the world as chronicled in the book of Genesis. In the opening, Haydn deftly creates a world of musical chaos whose dissonance is symbolically resolved by gentle melodies. Play this aria gently, and be mindful of the *crescendo* into the last measure.

The Lark

Composed in 1790, this charming and popular work was originally part of a string quartet. It was dedicated to his friend and benefactor Johann Tost, a Hungarian violinist. The tempo marking calls for a slow, sweet, and singing performance (*Adagio cantabile e dolce*).

Adagio cantabile e dolce

Symphony no. 59 "Fire"

This symphony was nicknamed "Fire" because excerpts of it were used in the play *Der Feuersbrunst* ("The Blaze"). As with most nicknames of symphonies, it was attached long after Haydn's time. Be mindful of the G#'s—they serve as leading tones to A in this minor key.

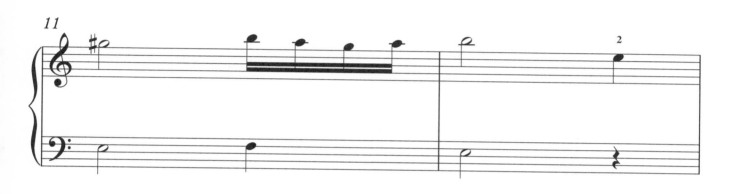

Piano Trio no. 34 in Bb Mvt. II

Andante cantabile asks the performer to play at a walking pace and in a song-like manner. Be expressive and link notes together as in a phrase. Use the chromatic notes in measures 2, 3, 4, and 6 (D#-G#-A#-D#) to add expression by leaning into the next note.

Andante cantabile

Et Incarnatus

from Mass No. 9 in C Major (Heiligmesse)

This mass was composed in honor of Saint Bernard of Offida, one of the patron saints of the noble Esterházy family (who commissioned Haydn). It is also known as the *Heiligmesse*, a name derived from the German translation of Sanctus, *Heilig*. This excerpt is taken from the Credo, and should be performed in a slow and contemplative manner.

Adagio

Piano Trio no. 45 in EB Mvt. II

The tempo marking for this movement is quite unique: *Andantino ed innocentemente* which means "at a leisurely pace and in an innocent manner." There is a playful relationship between the G# and G natural in the melody. Use this contrast to highlight the "innocent manner" of the work.

Andantino ed innocentemente

Gypsy Rondo

This melody is taken from the final movement of Piano Trio no. 39. Like many other European composers, Haydn admired the music of Europe's wandering Gypsies (also known as *Roma*). The trio ends in a whirlwind of notes with the melody played faster and faster, just like a Gypsy dance.

Allegretto

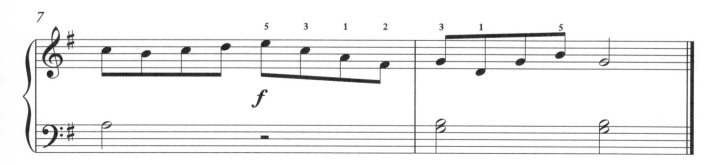

Keyboard Sonata no. 36 Mvt. II

Haydn is highly esteemed as a founder and pioneer of the Sonata form. Simply defined, it consists of three sections: an exposition, a development, and the restatement of the original theme. It was a hallmark of the Classical period, and marked a departure from structured Baroque forms.

Allegro moderato

Keyboard Sonata no. 11 Mvt. II

These series of works are referred to as *keyboard* rather than *piano* sonatas. Although the modern piano was premiered officially in 1709 (approximately 50 years before these compositions), the harpsichord and clavichord were still the standard household instruments. Music was published with this in mind, and the name stands to this day (although other genres such as trios have adopted the word *piano*).

Andante

Symphony no. 4 "Trauer"

The subtitle of this symphony (*Trauer*) means "mourning." It was written in 1772 and presents a refined expression for its time. Pay close attention to the dynamic contrasts: from forte (*f*) to piano (*p*), and mezzo-forte (*mf*) to pianissimo (*pp*). Also, the opening theme is highlighted by the use of octaves and should be played evenly between the two hands.

Allegro moderato

Symphony no. 49 "La passion" (Opening)

La passione ("The Passion") is a nickname added years after the symphony's premiere. It remains unclear if it derives from the nature of the music or some other association with the theater (as with other monikers). Play at a slow pace and with a sense of expression, being sure to keep the opening thirds clear and not muddled.

Adagio

Symphony no. 100 "Militaire" Mvt. II

"Militaire" is derived from the second movement of this symphony. Haydn used trumpet fanfares and extended percussion in his orchestration, evoking images of military bands and war. Play brightly and crisply, with brass and percussion ensembles in mind.

Allegretto

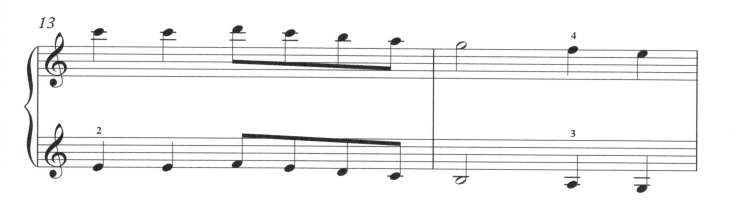

Piano Trio no. 24 Mvt. II

The second movement of this Piano Trio is in D minor (one flat), although the first movement is in D major (two sharps). Haydn creates contrast between the first and second movements by using the parallel minor key (D major to D minor), one of his many devices for creating structure. Play with feeling, keeping the thirds of the right hand clear.

Symphony no. 104 "London" (Opening)

This broad-shouldered symphony was composed in 1795 while Haydn was living in London. It is the final symphony he ever wrote. Play with confidence and emotion, and do not be tempted to play at a quick pace. Always be mindful of the *Adagio* marking, and contrast the character of the different sections.

Adagio

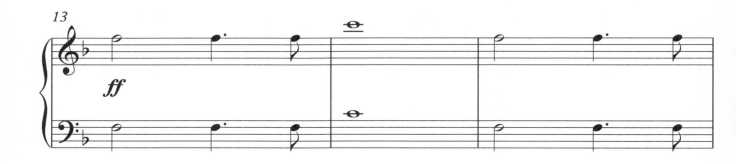

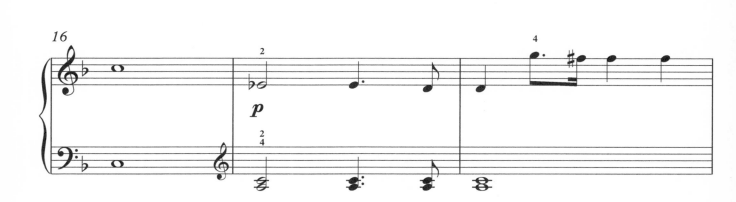

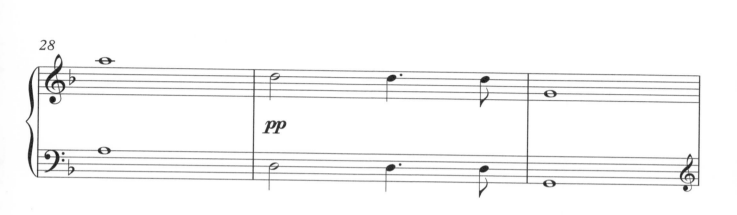

String Quartet no. 22 Mvt. II

Haydn wrote a total of 68 string quartets, and is known as the father of the genre. He was an avid string player and frequently performed in quartets with three of his closest friends: composers Johann Vanhal, Carl Ditters von Dittersdorf, and Wolfgang Amadeus Mozart. Play this excerpt with an emphasis on expressing dynamics.

Moderato

Adagio

Dynamic contrast is a large part of this work, and it represents a new phase in Haydn's music. This *Adagio i*s considered representative of the *Sturm und Drang* ("Storm and Stress") movement which brought new energy to music and to literature. It emphasized emotion and served as a precursor to Romanticism.

Adagio

Sonata in C

One of Haydn's most well-known works, it perfectly represents his sense of Classicism. The notes should be played detached and evenly, all creating an equal outline of the melody. The *diminuendo* in measure 10 is designed to give a smooth exit for theme by gradually reducing volume.

Moderato

Serenade from Strings Quartet op. 3, no. 5

This famous work is celebrated for its serenity and peaceful nature. It was originally written for a string quartet, although today it has been arranged for many ensembles. Be mindful of the sixteenth notes in measure 10: isolate and practice the phrase separately if you're having difficulty. It should sound just as even and lyrical as the rest of the work.

Musical Clock, no. 8

The original title for this collection was *Flötenuhrstücke*, and it consists of 17 pieces for a mechanical organ. Much like the piano rolls that would come later, the organs could be mechanically programmed. When playing, keep in mind the precision and unity of both voices that were created by these machines.

Moderato

Symphony no. 101 "Clock" Mvt. II

The term "Clock" was derived from the second movement of this symphony, where the music is scored for plucked strings and bassoons. The instrumentation and constant pulse reminded audiences of a ticking clock. Play difficult passages slowly until the tempo can reach that of the rest of the music.

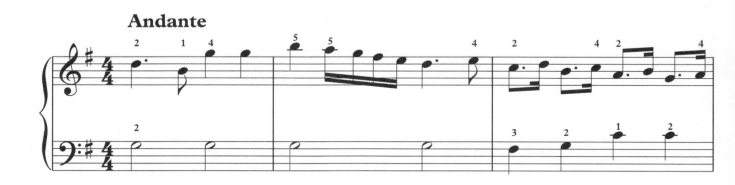